STUDENT GUIDE

# RATES, RATIOS, PROPORTIONS, AND PERCENTS

BUYER BEWARE

MathScape
SEEING AND THINKING
MATHEMATICALLY

# Buyer Beware

For best buys...

## How to:

- Compare Cost
- Compare Quantities
- Save with Coupons

## Also...

**Budget for a Banquet**

**Estimate Expenses**

To: Staff Reporters
From: Buyer Beware Magazine, Inc.

Welcome to Buyer Beware. As a staff reporter, your job is to help your readers become more educated consumers. Mathematics is an important part of consumer awareness. You will use unit pricing to find the better buy, write ratios to compare brands, and use proportions to increase recipes and determine cost. You will use percents to estimate discounts and interpret data in circle graphs.

# What math is involved in being an educated consumer?

# BUYER BEWARE

## PHASE**ONE**
### Rates

In this phase, you will compare the prices and sizes of products to determine which is the better buy. Next you will use a price graph to find and compare unit prices. Then you will decide when it is cheaper to buy by the pound. Finally, you will test claims made by a sandwich bar to see whether it is less expensive to buy a sandwich there or to make one at home.

## PHASE**TWO**
### Ratio and Proportion

You will begin this phase by writing ratios to compare quantities. Then you will use a ratio table to find equal ratios. Next, you will use equal ratios to compare brands. Then you will use proportions to increase a recipe. You will end the phase by using all that you have learned about ratio and proportion to plan an International Dinner.

## PHASE**THREE**
### Percents

You will begin this final phase by using familiar benchmarks, then counting and rounding to estimate expenses in a budget. Next, you will interpret and create circle graphs representing budgets for a drama club. Then you will use percents and discount coupons to find your savings in a percent-off sale. You will end the unit through a final activity: planning an athletic banquet on a budget.

# PHASE ONE

PHASE ONE

To: Staff Reporters

From: The Editors

Your first assignment is to test claims made about unit price. Super Sandwich Bar claims that it is less expensive to make a sandwich at their sandwich bar than it is to make one at home. When you complete the assignment we would like you to write an article for *Buyer Beware* stating your findings.

To prepare for this assignment, you will need some experience working with rates and unit prices.

Smart consumers want the best buy they can get for their money. To get the best buy, however, a consumer needs to look beyond advertised claims.

In order to do accurate comparison shopping, you need to know how to calculate unit price. By finding the unit price—the price per ounce, pound, or item—you will learn to make informed decisions and find the products that are better buys.

# Rates

## WHAT'S THE MATH?

*Investigations in this section focus on:*

### DATA and STATISTICS

- Finding unit prices using a price graph
- Constructing a price graph to compare unit prices

### NUMBER

- Comparing unit prices of different-size packages
- Comparing unit prices of different brands
- Finding the price per pound to decide the better buy
- Comparing prices per pound
- Calculating long-term savings
- Calculating unit prices and total prices

# What's the Best Buy?

**COMPARING UNIT PRICES**

**Shoppers need to be able to calculate unit prices to find the best buy.** In this lesson, you will compare various-size packages of cookies made by the same company to decide which size is the best buy. Then, you will compare two different brands of chocolate chip cookies to decide which one gives you more cookie for your money.

## Compare the Unit Prices of Different-Size Packages

**How can you compare cookie packages to find the best buy?**

The Buyer Beware Consumer Research Group has collected data on chocolate chip cookies. They want you to find out which package of Choco Chippies is the best buy.

To find the best buy, you need to find the unit price, or the price per cookie, for each size package. You can find the price of one cookie in a package if you know the total amount of cookies in the package and the price of the package.

**1** Use a calculator to figure out the price per cookie for each package. Round your answers to the nearest cent.

**2** Decide which package size is the best buy. Explain how you figured it out.

**3** List the different Choco Chippies package sizes in order from best buy to worst buy.

| Choco Chippies Prices | | |
|---|---|---|
| **Package Size** | **Number of Cookies** | **Package Price** |
| Snack | 4 | $0.50 |
| Regular | 17 | $1.39 |
| Family | 46 | $3.99 |
| Giant | 72 | $5.29 |

SNACK SIZE    REGULAR SIZE    FAMILY SIZE    GIANT SIZE

## Compare the Unit Prices of Two Different Brands

At *Buyer Beware* magazine we frequently get letters from our readers asking questions about best buys. Here is one of the letters we received:

> Dear Buyer Beware,
>
> Help! My friend and I don't agree on which brand of cookies is the best buy. She's convinced that it's Mini Chips, but I'm sure it's Duffy's Delights. Which is really the better buy?
>
> The Cookie Muncher

**How can you use unit price to determine which of two brands is the better buy?**

The research group at *Buyer Beware* has put together Cookie Prices data for you to use.

1. Decide which unit you would use to compare the two different brands of cookie. Explain why you chose that unit.

2. Find the price per unit of each brand of cookies.

3. Compare the unit price of the two brands of cookies. Is one brand the better buy? If so, explain why. If not, explain why the brands are equally good buys.

### Cookie Prices

| Brand | Package Price | Number of Cookies | Package Weight |
|---|---|---|---|
| Mini Chips | $1.39 | 17 | 6 oz |
| Duffy's Delights | $2.29 | 10 | 11 oz |

## Determine the Better Buy

Write a response letter to The Cookie Muncher.

- Describe what you did to figure out the better buy.

- Give evidence to support your conclusions.

- Give some general tips for finding the best buy.

MINI CHIPS          DUFFY'S DELIGHT

*hot* **words** | unit price rate

 page 34

# 2 The Best Snack Bar Bargain

**You can use a price graph to compare unit prices for different products.** In this lesson you will use a price graph to determine the price at different quantities of a snack bar if you were paying by the ounce. Then you will construct a price graph to compare the prices of five different products.

## Use a Price Graph to Find Unit Price

**How can you use a price graph to estimate snack bar prices?**

The graph below shows the prices for three different snack bars. The price of Mercury Bars is $1.00 for 2 oz. Jupiter Bars are $2.98 for 3.5 oz and Saturn Bars are $3.50 for 4.5 oz.

Each of the three dots on the graph shows the price and the number of ounces for one of the snack bars. Each line shows the price of different quantities of the snack bar at the same price per ounce.

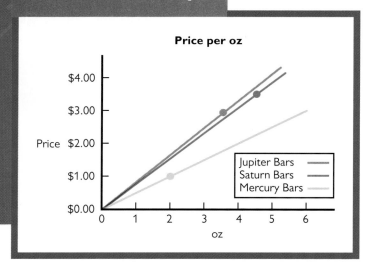

**Snack Bar Line Graph**

Price per oz

Legend:
- Jupiter Bars
- Saturn Bars
- Mercury Bars

**1** Use the price graph to find the price of a 3-oz Mercury Bar.

**2** Use the price graph to find the price of a 0.5-oz Saturn Bar.

**3** Use the price graph to find which snack bar has the lowest unit price and which has the highest unit price.

**4** Use your calculator to find the unit price of 1 oz of each of the snack bars. Use the price graph to check your calculations.

## Construct a Price Graph to Compare Unit Prices

The Buyer Beware research group has collected data on five different products.

**How can you use a price graph to compare product prices?**

| Product | Number of Units | Price |
|---------|-----------------|-------|
| Oatmeal | 14 oz | $2.40 |
| Tuna | 7.5 oz | $2.00 |
| Penne pasta | 8 oz | $1.00 |
| Sourdough pretzels | 12 oz | $2.60 |
| Whole wheat rolls | 9 oz | $1.60 |

**1** Use the above data to construct a price graph.

**2** Use the price graph to complete a Price Comparison. For each product, record the price for 1 oz, 3 oz, 4.5 oz, and 6 oz.

### Price Comparison Table

| Product | 1 oz | 3 oz | 4.5 oz | 6 oz |
|---------|------|------|--------|------|
| Oatmeal | | | | |
| | | | | |
| | | | | |

**3** Which product is the most expensive per ounce? the least expensive per ounce?

## Write About Your Price Graph

Think about what you have learned about interpreting and making price graphs.

- Write a description of your price graph and what it shows. Explain how to use your price graph to find prices for packages that are larger and smaller than your original package.

- Describe how two products will look on a price graph if their prices are almost the same per ounce.

*hot* **words** | unit price
rate

page 35

# 3 Cheaper by the Pound

**USING UNIT PRICES AND WEIGHT UNITS TO COMPARE PRICES**

**Sometimes buying in "bulk" or larger quantities will save you money.** In this lesson you will find the price per pound of different-size packages of rice to decide which one is the best buy. Then you will evaluate the price per pound of items at a silly sale.

## Find the Price per Pound to Decide the Best Buy

**How can you find the package that is the least expensive per pound?**

**1** What is the price per pound of each package of rice? Round your answer to the nearest cent.

**2** Find out which package of rice is the best buy in terms of price per pound.

**3** Explain which package of rice makes the most sense to buy if only one person in a family eats rice.

**4** Decide which package of rice would be the best buy for your family.

| Fluffy Rice | |
|---|---|
| 2 lbs | $1.09 |
| 5 lbs | $2.69 |
| 10 lbs | $4.99 |
| 20 lbs | $7.99 |

2 POUNDS
$1.09

5 POUNDS
$2.69

10 POUNDS
$4.99

20 POUNDS
$7.99

## Compare Prices per Pound

Suppose you go to a silly sale where everything is rated by price per pound. Which is cheapest per pound: a bicycle, a pair of sneakers, a video camera, or a refrigerator?

**How can you determine the prices per pound of different items?**

43 POUNDS
$139.99

2 POUNDS
$84.99

11 POUNDS
$799.00

230 POUNDS
$679.99

**1** Use your calculator to find the price per pound of each item.

**2** Rank the items from the least to most expensive per pound.

**3** What items have high prices per pound?

**4** What items have low prices per pound?

## Write About Buying in Bulk

Write what you know about buying in bulk. Be sure to answer these questions in your writing:

- How can you figure out if the largest size is the least expensive per pound?

- Is the largest size always the least expensive per pound?

- When is it a good idea to buy products in bulk? When is it not a good idea?

- Could the same purchase be a good choice for one consumer but not for another consumer? Explain.

*hot* **words** | unit price
rate

page 36

# 4 It Really Adds Up

SOLVING REAL-LIFE
PROBLEMS AND
FINDING THE
BETTER BUY

**In this lesson you will use what you have learned about unit prices to solve real-life problems.** First, you will decide the savings on two different brands of pretzels. Then you will take on the role of an investigative reporter to test the claim made by a sandwich bar.

## Calculate Long-Term Savings

**How much can you save over time by buying a less expensive brand?**

People are often surprised at how buying a little snack every day can really add up over time. The Buyer Beware research team wants you to figure out the price of buying two brands of pretzels for different time periods.

**1** Find the price of buying one bag of pretzels every day for a week, a month, and a year. Make a table like the one below to organize your answers.

**2** How much would you save if you bought No-Ad Pretzels instead of Crunchy Pretzels for the different time periods?

**3** If you bought a bag of No-Ad Pretzels every day instead of Crunchy Pretzels, how many days would it take to save $30? $75? Explain how you figured it out.

### Pretzel Costs

| Type of Pretzels | Price for 1 Bag a Day for 1 Day | Price for 1 Bag a Day for 1 Week | Price for 1 Bag a Day for 1 Month (4.3 weeks) | Price for 1 Bag a Day for 1 Year |
|---|---|---|---|---|
| Crunchy Pretzels | $0.65 | | | |
| No-Ad Pretzels | $0.50 | | | |
| Savings for buying No-Ad Pretzels | | | | |

## Calculate Unit Prices and Total Prices

At Super Sandwich Bar, customers can make their own Terrific Ten Sandwich—two slices of cheese and eight slices of meat—for only $3.59. The restaurant claims that this is cheaper than making the sandwich at home. The Buyer Beware research group wants you to test this claim. They have collected information on the prices of different ingredients for you to use.

**How can you test a claim by figuring out unit prices?**

### Sandwich Tips

STEPS TO DESIGNING A SUPER SANDWICH

**1.** Choose *at least* three ingredients from the handout In Search of the Terrific Ten Sandwich.

**2.** Make a table. List the ingredients you chose, the amount of each, and the price of each.

**3.** What is the total price of your giant sandwich if you paid for it by the slice?

**4.** Do you think Super Sandwich Bar's price of $3.59 is a good deal? Explain your reasoning.

**5.** Name your sandwich and draw a picture of it for a magazine article.

## Write About Super Sandwich Bar's Claims

- Describe the strategies and solutions you used to figure out the total price of your sandwich.

- Write a magazine article discussing your findings about the claims made by Super Sandwich Bar. In your article answer the question: Is it cheaper to make a sandwich at the bar or buy all the ingredients and make it yourself?

*hot* **words** | unit price

page 37

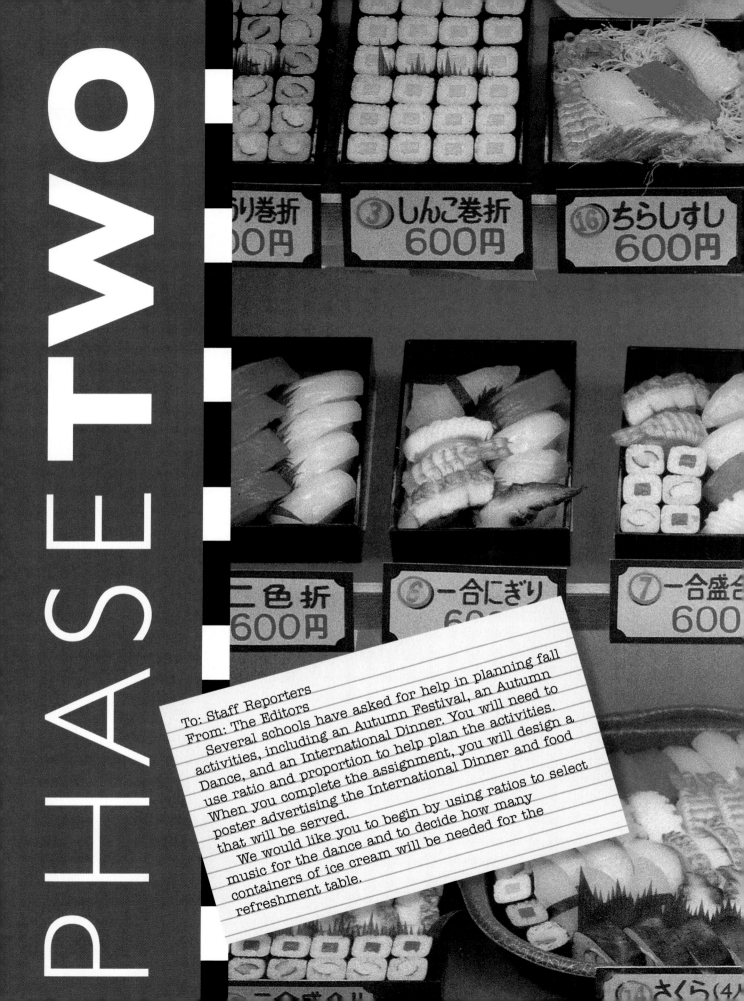

PHASE TWO

③ しんこ巻折
600円

⑯ ちらしすし
600円

り巻折
00円

二色折
600円

⑥ 一合にぎり
60

⑦ 一合盛合
600

さくら（4）

To: Staff Reporters
From: The Editors
    Several schools have asked for help in planning fall activities, including an Autumn Festival, an Autumn Dance, and an International Dinner. You will need to use ratio and proportion to help plan the activities. When you complete the assignment, you will design a poster advertising the International Dinner and food that will be served.
    We would like you to begin by using ratios to select music for the dance and to decide how many containers of ice cream will be needed for the refreshment table.

Can ratio and proportion be useful in planning school activities? A ratio is a relationship between two quantities of the same measure. Ratios are useful when you want to compare data, decide quantities of servings, or compare different products.

A proportion states that two ratios are equal. Setting up and solving a proportion can help you increase recipes or plan amounts of ingredients needed for a meal.

# Ratio and Proportion

## WHAT'S THE MATH?

*Investigations in this section focus on:*

### NUMBER

- Using ratios to compare data
- Using equivalent fractions to compare ratios

### SCALE and PROPORTION

- Finding equal ratios with a ratio table
- Using cross products to compare ratios
- Using equal ratios and cross products to solve proportions
- Using proportions to increase a recipe
- Using proportions to decide cost

# 5 Dancing Ratios

**A ratio is a comparison of one number to another.**
In this lesson you will use ratios to select music for a dance. Then you will use a ratio table to determine how many containers of ice cream are needed for the refreshment table at the dance.

## Use Ratios to Compare Data

**How can ratios help you compare survey results?**

The members of the music committee at Brown Middle School conducted a survey to select the music they will play at the Autumn Dance. They asked 150 students to name their favorite dance music. The graph below shows the results of the survey.

Use the graph to answer the questions. Write your answers in lowest terms. A ratio compares two numbers. You can write a ratio as a fraction. The ratio $\frac{6}{12}$ can be written in lowest terms as $\frac{1}{2}$. This ratio can also be written as $1:2$.

**1** What is the ratio of votes for the least popular music choice to votes for the most popular?

**2** Which preferences does each ratio compare?

   a. $\frac{3}{5}$    b. $\frac{4}{9}$    c. $\frac{1}{3}$

**3** Conduct a music survey in your math class. Use the same music choices as the ones on the graph. Write ratios to compare results.

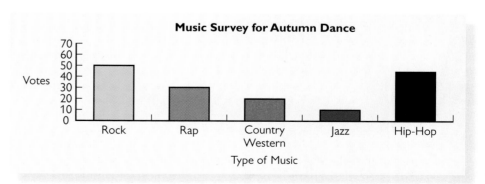

## Find Equal Ratios with a Ratio Table

The refreshment committee plans to serve ice cream at the dance. Each container of ice cream serves eight students. How many containers of ice cream are needed for 96 students? A ratio table can help you solve this problem.

**How can you use a ratio table to determine how much ice cream to buy?**

| Ice cream containers | 1 | 2 | 3 | 4 | 5 |
|---|---|---|---|---|---|
| Servings | 8 | 16 | 24 | | |

**1** Complete the table for four and five ice cream containers.

**2** Extend the table to figure out how many containers you would need for 96 student servings.

**3** Find two methods to show that the ratios are equivalent.

## Write About Ratios

Think about the ways in which you used ratios in this lesson. Use the following questions to help you write what you know about ratios.

- What is a ratio?
- What can ratios tell you?
- Why is it useful to express ratios in lowest terms?

*hot* **words** | ratio
equivalent fractions

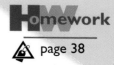

page 38

# 6 Which Brand Has the Most Chocolate?

**COMPARING RATIOS**

**You can use equivalent fractions and cross products to compare ratios.** In this lesson you will use equivalent fractions to compare brands of trail mix. Then you will use cross products to decide which brand of popcorn pops to fill more cups.

## Use Equivalent Fractions to Compare Ratios

**How can comparing fractions help you decide which trail mix to buy?**

Dwight Middle School is planning an Autumn Festival. The seventh grade is planning to buy trail mix to sell at the festival. They want to decide if one of two brands, Mountain Trail Mix or Hiker's Trail Mix, contains more chocolate by weight or if both contain the same amount. The *Buyer Beware* research group has collected the information shown on the two brands. Note: The mixes contain only dried fruit and chocolate chips.

**1** What is the ratio of chocolate chips to dried fruit by weight in Mountain Trail Mix?

**2** What is the ratio of chocolate chips to dried fruit by weight in Hiker's Trail Mix?

**3** Are the ratios of chocolate chips to dried fruit for each type of mix the same or different?

| **Mountain Trail Mix** |
| 6 oz chocolate chips |
| 10 oz dried fruit |
| |
| **Hiker's Trail Mix** |
| 4 oz chocolate chips |
| 6 oz dried fruit |

**4** Does one trail mix brand contain more chocolate per ounce than the other? If so, which one? How do you know?

### Equal Ratios

Two ratios are equal if the fractions formed are equivalent. For example, the ratios 2:4 and 8:16 are equal because the fractions are equivalent ($\frac{2}{4} = \frac{8}{16}$). The ratios 2:4 and 8:15 are not equal because $\frac{2}{4} \neq \frac{8}{15}$.

## Use Cross Products to Compare Ratios

The seventh grade at Dwight Middle School is planning to sell popcorn at the Autumn Festival. They want to buy the brand of uncooked popcorn that will yield the most cooked popcorn. The *Buyer Beware* research group collected the information shown on two different brands of uncooked popcorn: Speedy Popcorn and Crunchy Popcorn.

You can use cross products to compare ratios. If the cross products are equal, the ratios are equal.

> **Speedy Popcorn**
> 1 cup uncooked popcorn makes 5 cups cooked popcorn.
>
> **Crunchy Popcorn**
> 4 cups uncooked popcorn makes 25 cups cooked popcorn.

**1** Which brand gives you the best ratio of uncooked popcorn to cooked popcorn or are they both the same?

**2** For each brand, how many cups of uncooked popcorn do you need to make 100 cups of cooked popcorn?

**3** Another brand has a ratio of uncooked to cooked popcorn of 4:15. Yet another brand has a ratio of uncooked to cooked of 5:20. How do the ratios compare? Explain.

## Compare Brands

Write a letter to the Dwight Middle School seventh grade class. Include the following:

- Give your advice about which brand of popcorn to buy. Explain the reason behind your recommendation.

- Tell what math you used to solve the problem.

> **How can using cross products help you make buying decisions?**

*hot* **words** | equivalent ratios
cross products

page 39

# 7 Halftime Refreshments

SOLVING
PROPORTIONS

**In this lesson, you will use proportions to decide how many spoonfuls of hot cocoa mix are needed to make mugs of hot cocoa.** Then you will use proportions to increase a brownie recipe.

## Use Equal Ratios and Cross Products

**How can you use what you know to solve a proportion?**

The seventh grade is planning to sell mugs full of hot cocoa at the football game. If 6 spoonfuls of hot cocoa mix make 3 mugs of hot cocoa, how many spoonfuls are needed to make 9 mugs?

To solve problems like this, you can set up and solve a proportion, such as the one shown below. A proportion shows that two ratios are equal.

$$\frac{6 \text{ spoonfuls}}{3 \text{ mugs}} = \frac{n \text{ spoonfuls}}{9 \text{ mugs}}$$

**1** Write a proportion to show how many spoonfuls would be needed for each of the following:

    **a.** 21 mugs       **b.** 36 mugs       **c.** 95 mugs

**2** How many mugs could you make with 360 spoonfuls of cocoa mix?

**3** Explain how you set up and solved the proportion.

### Two Ways to Solve a Proportion

| Equal Ratios | Cross Products |
|---|---|
| $\frac{6 \times 3}{3 \times 3} = \frac{n}{9}$ | $\frac{6}{3} = \frac{n}{9}$ |
| $6 \times 3 = n$ | $3 \times n = 6 \times 9$ |
| $18 = n$ | $3n = 54$ |
| | $n = 18$ |

## Use Proportions to Increase a Recipe

The refreshment committee plans to sell brownies at the school football game. They plan to use the following brownie recipe. Each member of the committee needs to bake 20 large brownies. How would you increase the recipe to make 20 large brownies?

**How can you use proportions to measure ingredients?**

**1** Write and solve a proportion that shows how much of each ingredient in the recipe would be needed to make:

**a.** 30 brownies **b.** 70 brownies **c.** 100 brownies

### Rocky Mountain Chocolate Chip Brownies

5 oz unsalted butter
2 oz margarine
8 oz dark brown sugar
6 oz granulated sugar
2 oz milk
2 eggs

16 oz sifted flour
10 oz semi-sweet chocolate chips
8 oz chopped walnuts
1 oz baking powder
1 oz vanilla extract
1 oz baking soda

Makes 8 large brownies

**2** Explain how to set up the proportions.

**3** Explain how you solved the proportions.

## Write About Proportions

Write about how you used proportions in this lesson. Include answers to the following questions:

- What is a proportion?

- Which proportions did you solve using equal ratios? using cross products?

- Is it sometimes easier to solve a proportion using cross products rather than equal ratios? Explain why.

*hot* **words** | proportion
cross products

Homework

page 40

# 8 A **Proportional** Buffet

USING RATIO AND
PROPORTION TO
SOLVE PROBLEMS

**In this lesson, you will apply all that you have learned about ratio and proportion to help you plan an International Dinner.** First, you will choose a recipe and increase it to serve more people. Then, you will choose appetizers and use proportions to decide their total cost.

## Set Up and Solve Proportions

**How can proportions help you plan an event?**

Brown Middle School is planning an International Dinner. The seventh grade has been given a choice of four recipes to make for the dinner. They need to know how to increase each recipe to serve 20 people.

**1** Choose *one* recipe from the handout International Dinner Recipes.

**2** Use proportions to increase the recipe to serve 20 people. Make 1 serving per person.

**3** Explain the math you used to solve this problem.

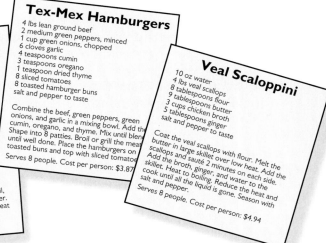

**African Peanut Soup**

1 tablespoon butter
4 oz chopped onion
1 tablespoon ginger
3 oz chopped peanuts
16 oz chicken stock
4 oz raisins
1 tablespoon honey
3 oz peanut butter
8 oz milk
1 teaspoon cinnamon
salt and pepper to taste

Sauté onion, ginger, salt, and pepper in butter until onions become clear. Add cinnamon and peanuts and sauté 5–10 minutes. Stir in chicken stock, raisins, honey, and peanut butter. Mix thoroughly. Cover and simmer over low heat for one hour. Add milk and serve when soup is hot.

Serves 8 people. Cost per person: $1.79

**Spanish Seafood Gazpacho**

2 cups fresh bread crumbs
3 cloves minced garlic
1 medium cucumber, peeled and diced
2 medium sweet red peppers, chopped
3 small jalapeño peppers, chopped
1 medium red onion, chopped
5 medium ripe tomatoes, diced
5 cups tomato juice
4 oz olive oil
2 cups crab meat
1 medium avocado, diced
juice of 4 limes
salt and pepper to taste

Combine bread crumbs and garlic. Add the cucumber, red peppers, jalapeño peppers, onion, and tomato. Pour in tomato juice, oil, and lime juice. Purée ingredients in a blender. Season with salt and pepper. Stir in crab meat and avocado.

Serves 8 people. Cost per person: $3.15

**Tex-Mex Hamburgers**

4 lbs lean ground beef
2 medium green peppers, minced
1 cup green onions, chopped
6 cloves garlic
4 teaspoons cumin
3 teaspoons oregano
1 teaspoon dried thyme
8 sliced tomatoes
8 toasted hamburger buns
salt and pepper to taste

Combine the beef, green peppers, green onions, and garlic in a mixing bowl. Add the cumin, oregano, and thyme. Mix until blended. Shape into 8 patties. Broil or grill the meat until well done. Place the hamburgers on toasted buns and top with sliced tomatoes.

Serves 8 people. Cost per person: $3.87

**Veal Scaloppini**

10 oz water
4 lbs veal scallops
8 tablespoons flour
8 tablespoons butter
3 cups chicken broth
5 tablespoons ginger
salt and pepper to taste

Coat the veal scallops with flour. Melt the butter in large skillet over low heat. Add the scallops and sauté 2 minutes on each side. Add the broth, ginger, and water to the skillet. Heat to boiling. Reduce the heat and cook until all the liquid is gone. Season with salt and pepper.

Serves 8 people. Cost per person: $4.94

## Use a Proportion to Decide Costs

The parent association has decided to purchase a variety of appetizers for the International Dinner. Use the handout International Dinner Appetizer Costs to help you make your choices for the appetizer buffet.

**How can you use what you have learned to predict costs?**

**1** Use the handout to select five different appetizer plates. For each appetizer you chose, find the cost to serve 20 people.

**2** Record your selections and their costs in a chart like the one here.

**International Dinner Appetizer Costs**

|   | Appetizer | Cost | Cost for 20 People |
|---|-----------|------|--------------------|
| 1. |           |      |                    |
| 2. |           |      |                    |
| 3. |           |      |                    |
| 4. |           |      |                    |
| 5. |           |      |                    |

## Write About Cost and Value

Figure out what the charge per person for the International Dinner should be to cover the food expenses.

- Write about how you decided what the price of admission should be.

- Make a poster advertising the International Dinner. On the poster include the price of admission to the event. Include descriptions of the featured foods, entertainment, and activities to convince someone that the dinner is worth the price.

*hot* **words** | proportion
ratio

H**omework**

page 41

# PHASE THREE

To: Staff Reporters

From: The Editors

Your final assignment is to plan an athletic banquet on a budget. A budget is the amount of money that is available for a particular use. When you complete the assignment you will write a magazine article for Buyer Beware on "Planning a Banquet on a Budget."

To prepare for this assignment, you will need to get some experience working with percents.

In this final phase you will use percents to help you become a smart shopper. Knowing about percents will help you to interpret discounts and resulting sale prices. If you know how much the discount actually reduces the price of an item, you can make informed decisions about what to buy and what not to buy.

# Percents

## WHAT'S THE MATH?

*Investigations in this section focus on:*

### NUMBER

- Estimating expenses
- Exploring counting and rounding
- Calculating discounts
- Following a budget
- Determining savings
- Estimating and calculating percents

### DATA and STATISTICS

- Interpreting a circle graph

### GEOMETRY and MEASUREMENT

- Constructing a circle graph

# 9 Team Spirit

**In this lesson you will use benchmarks and mental math to estimate the expenses of a football team.** Then you will count and round to estimate the amount of money a field hockey team must raise to travel to a tournament.

## Estimate Expenses

**How can you use benchmarks to help you estimate expenses?**

Estimating a percent of something is much the same as estimating a fractional part of something.

Last year the Cougars' football team's total expenses were $20,000. The table below shows what percent of the budget was spent on each expense. About how much money was spent on each item?

**1** Make a table like the one shown below and complete the last column. Estimate the cost of each expense. Use benchmarks and mental math to make your estimates. Do not use paper and pencil.

**2** The team spent exactly $800 on one expense. Which was it? Use estimation to figure it out.

**3** The Tigers football team, cross-town rivals, spent 26% of its $16,000 budget on uniforms. Which team spent more on uniforms? Use estimation to figure it out.

### Football Team Expenses

| Items | Percent of Budget | Estimated Cost |
|-------|-------------------|----------------|
| Uniforms | 23% | |
| Transportation | 6% | |
| Coach's salary | 48% | |
| Equipment | 11% | |
| Officials' fees | 4% | |
| Trainer's salary | 8% | |
| **Total Expenses:** | | **$20,000** |

## Explore Counting and Rounding

A girls' field hockey team wants to play in a tournament. The school district will pay only a certain percentage of each expense. The team must raise the amount not paid by the district.

If you can find 50%, 10%, and 1% of a number mentally, you can also estimate some other percents mentally. For example, think of 25% as half of 50% and 5% as half of 10%.

### Field Hockey Team Trip Expenses

| Expense | Estimated Cost | Percent District Will Pay |
|---|---|---|
| Transportation | $700 | 3% |
| Meals | $600 | 12% |
| Hotel | $925 | 4% |
| Tournament fees | $346 | 22% |
| Tournament uniforms | $473 | 2.5% |

**1** Use counting and rounding to estimate the dollar amount the school district will pay for each expense.

**2** Estimate the total amount the district will pay for all the expenses.

**3** Estimate the total amount of money the team will need to raise.

**4** Use your calculator to figure out the exact amount the team will need to raise for each expense.

## Write About Your Estimates

Write about the estimates you made for the field hockey team expenses.

- What strategies did you use to estimate the expenses and total cost?

- What are some ways to determine whether your estimate is reasonable?

hot words    percent benchmark

Homework

page 42

# 10 Playing Around

**Circle graphs are useful tools for comparing percents.** They show how different parts are related to a whole. In this lesson you will use a calculator to analyze data in a circle graph. Then you will use survey information about fund-raisers to make your own circle graph.

## Use a Calculator to Find Percents in a Circle Graph

**How can you analyze data in a circle graph?**

The drama club plans to present a production of Moss Hart's *You Can't Take It With You*. The cost of the production is displayed in the following circle graph.

**1** What is the total cost of the production? Use the circle graph to estimate what percent of the total cost was spent on each expense. Tip: Compare the size of each section to the whole circle.

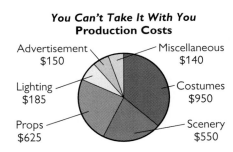

**You Can't Take It With You Production Costs**

Advertisement $150
Miscellaneous $140
Lighting $185
Costumes $950
Props $625
Scenery $550

**2** Use your calculator to help you find the percent of each expense in the circle graph. First, find the percent that will be spent on costumes by expressing the amount as a fraction; for example:

$$\frac{\text{cost of costumes}}{\text{total cost of production}}$$

Then, change the fraction into a decimal. Use your calculator to help you with this. Divide the cost of the costumes by the total cost of the production. To express the decimal as a percent, multiply the decimal by 100, round to the nearest whole number, and add a percent (%) sign.

**3** Compare your estimates with the exact percent you got using the calculator. How close were your estimates?

# Construct a Circle Graph

The drama club decided it would like to attend a performance of Andrew Lloyd Webber's *Cats*. In order to see the musical production, they needed to raise the money to purchase the tickets. They conducted a survey in the middle school to find out which type of fund-raiser most students would be likely to attend. The survey gave the following results.

**How can you construct a circle graph to show survey results?**

**Fund-Raiser Choices by Number of Students in Each Grade**

| Choice | 6th Grade Students | 7th Grade Students | 8th Grade Students | Total Students | Percent of Students |
|---|---|---|---|---|---|
| Carnival | 88 | 75 | 69 | | |
| Raffle | 45 | 49 | 41 | | |
| Car wash | 66 | 54 | 52 | | |
| Bake sale | 34 | 32 | 33 | | |
| Candy sale | 12 | 11 | 15 | | |
| Don't know | 3 | 4 | 1 | | |

**1** Figure out the total number of students who were surveyed.

**2** Use your calculator to find the percent of students in the middle school that chose each activity. Round your answers to the nearest whole number.

**3** Follow the guidelines on the handout Circle Graph to help you construct a circle graph to display your data.

# Conduct Your Own Survey

Conduct a survey in your math class to find out which fund-raiser your classmates would choose to attend.

- Figure out what percent of the class chose each type of fund-raiser.

- Make a circle graph to represent your class's survey results.

- Compare your class's results to the data in the table.

*hot* **words** | circle graph
angle

page 43

# 11 Sale Daze

USING PERCENTS
TO CALCULATE
SALE PRICES AND
DISCOUNTS

**Buying items on sale is a great way to save money.**
In this lesson you will calculate your savings by purchasing a skateboard at a percent-off sale. Then you will use discount coupons to shop for sporting equipment.

## Determine Savings

**How can you calculate your savings in a percent-off sale?**

You want to join the after-school skateboard club this year, but you need to purchase the required equipment in order to participate. Skates on Seventh is advertising a percent-off sale. You have $175 to spend. Refer to this advertisement in answering the following questions.

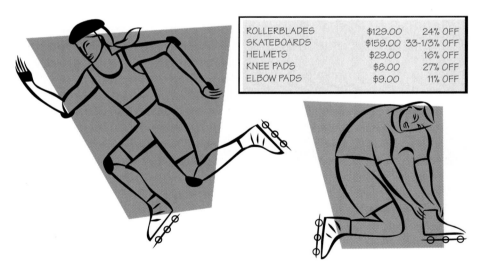

| ROLLERBLADES | $129.00 | 24% OFF |
| SKATEBOARDS | $159.00 | 33-1/3% OFF |
| HELMETS | $29.00 | 16% OFF |
| KNEE PADS | $8.00 | 27% OFF |
| ELBOW PADS | $9.00 | 11% OFF |

**1** Make a quick estimate to see if you have enough money to buy a skateboard, helmet, knee pads, and elbow pads.

**2** Use your calculator to figure out how much you will save for each item.

**3** Figure out the sale price of each item.

## Shop with Discount Coupons

The sports club wants to buy a variety of sports equipment for students to try out. They want you to buy as many new pieces of equipment as you can for their budget of $350. Fortunately, they have lots of discount coupons for you to use.

You need to buy *at least* three different kinds of equipment and use a different coupon from the handout Discount Coupons for each one. Remember, you can use each coupon only once and you can't use more than one coupon per type of equipment. The goal is to spend close to $350 without going over.

**How much money will you save by shopping with discount coupons?**

**1** Decide which items you want to buy and which coupons you will use for each.

**2** Make a table to show each original cost, the discount from the coupon, and the sale price.

**3** Figure out the total cost of your purchases.

**4** Figure out how much you saved by buying the items with discount coupons.

| | |
|---|---|
| BASKETBALL | $23.00 |
| CHAMPIONSHIP BASKETBALL | $52.00 |
| VOLLEYBALL | $44.00 |
| VOLLEYBALL NET | $109.00 |
| CATCHER'S MITT | $51.50 |
| CATCHER'S MASK | $15.70 |
| BASEBALLS | $39.50 PER DOZEN |
| BASEBALL BAT | $26.95 |
| BATTING HELMET | $11.85 |
| SOCCER BALL | $26.30 |
| TENNIS RACKET | $49.55 |
| TENNIS BALLS | $12.00 FOR 3 CANS |
| FOOTBALL | $18.00 |
| HOCKEY STICK | $49.00 |
| HOCKEY PUCK | 14.00 FOR 2 |

## Design a Sale Advertisement

Create a colorful flyer announcing a sale at your favorite department store. For each advertised item, include:

- the original price
- the percent off, discount, and sale price

*hot* **words** | discount price

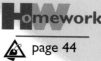

**H**omework

page 44

# 12 Percent Smorgasbord

**A budget is a useful tool for keeping track of your money.** In this lesson you will be given a set amount of money to plan an athletic banquet. You will need to plan a menu, select entertainment, and purchase awards, decorations, and gifts for the coaches. Finally, you will use all of your data to display your budget in a circle graph.

## Use a Budget to Plan an Athletic Banquet

**How can you work with a budget to make planning decisions?**

You have been given $2,500 to plan the athletic banquet. The money was donated for the banquet and that's all it can be used for, so you need to spend close to $2,500. You can't spend more than this.

**Athletic Banquet Attendance**

| Sport | Students | Coaches |
|---|---|---|
| Field hockey | 20 | 2 |
| Football | 50 | 3 |
| Soccer | 30 | 2 |
| Tennis | 16 | 2 |
| Basketball | 20 | 2 |
| Volleyball | 12 | 1 |
| Cross-country | 12 | 1 |
| Swimming | 8 | 1 |
| Lacrosse | 18 | 2 |

1 Use the handout Athletic Banquet Price List to help you plan your choices for food, entertainment, awards, decorations, and gifts for the coaches.

2 When you have figured out how much you will spend for each category, write your plan for what you will be doing for each of the following: food, entertainment, awards, decorations, and gifts for the coaches.

3 Make a chart to record your total expenses in each category.

4 Write down the total amount you will spend on the banquet. Tell how much money, if any, you will have left over from the $2,500 you were given to spend.

## Display Your Budget Data in a Circle Graph

You need to present the information in your banquet plan to the athletic advisory committee. Make a circle graph for the presentation.

- Use the circle on the handout Circle Graph.

- Use percents to label each sector of your circle graph.

- Make sure your sectors are clearly labeled and that the graph has a title.

### How can you make a budget presentation?

## Write an Article for *Buyer Beware*

Write an article for *Buyer Beware* magazine called "A Banquet on a Budget."

- Your article should include your chart and circle graph.

- Include tips to readers on how to make choices that save money.

hot **words** | budget
circle graph

omework

 page 45

# What's the Best Buy?

## Applying Skills

Use your calculator to find the unit price for each of the following. Round to the nearest cent.

**1.** 7 oz of crackers for $1.19

**2.** 14 oz of cottage cheese for $1.19

**3.** 16 boxes of raisins for $5.60

Find the better buy based on unit price.

**4.** A 35-oz can of Best Brand Plum Tomatoes is on sale for $0.69. A 4-lb can of Sun Ripe Plum Tomatoes is $1.88.

**5.** A can of Favorite Dog Food holds 14 oz. Four cans are $1.00. The price of three cans of Delight Beef Dog Food, each containing 12 oz, is $0.58.

**6.** For each item, predict which is the better buy. Then use paper and pencil or a calculator to find the better buy.

| | Item | Jefferson Auto Stores | Tom's Auto Parts |
|---|---|---|---|
| **a.** | oil | 12 qt for $10.99 | 6 qt for $5.99 |
| **b.** | antifreeze | 12 oz for $3.79 | 6 oz for $1.79 |
| **c.** | auto wax | 6 cans for $14.29 | 5 cans for $12.98 |

## Extending Concepts

**7.** Six cans of fruit drink are on sale for $1.95. Individually, the price of each can is $0.35. How much does Tanya save buying 6 cans on sale?

**8.** Tubes of oil paint can be bought in sets of 5 for $13.75 or bought separately for the unit price. What would be the price of 2 tubes of this oil paint?

**9.** The price of three bottles of Bright Shine Window Cleaner, each containing 15 oz, is $2.75. Two bottles of Sparkle Window Cleaner, each containing 18 oz, can be purchased for $1.98. Which is the better buy?

## Writing

**10.** Create an advertisement for orange juice in which a small-size carton on sale is a better buy than a larger-size carton at regular price.

# The Best Snack Bar Bargain

## Applying Skills

The price graph below shows the unit prices for three different shampoos. Aloe Shampoo is $1.00 for 2 oz, Squeaky Clean is $2.75 for 3.5 oz, and Shine So Soft is $3.75 for 4 oz.

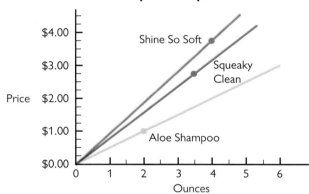

**Shampoo Price per Ounce**

1. Use the graph to find the price of 4 oz of Aloe Shampoo.

2. Use the graph to find the price of 0.5 oz of Shine So Soft.

3. Use the graph to find out which shampoo has the lowest unit price.

4. Use the graph to find out which shampoo has the highest unit price.

5. Use your calculator to find the price of 1 oz of each shampoo. Use the graph to check your calculations.

## Extending Concepts

Use the data from the products listed below to construct a price graph.

| Product | Number of Units | Price |
|---------|-----------------|-------|
| Crunchy Crackers | 9.5 oz | $1.20 |
| Buzzy Tuna | 5.5 oz | $1.00 |
| Bessy's Pancake Mix | 12 oz | $1.60 |
| Pino's Imported Pasta | 8 oz | $2.00 |
| Lean ground beef | 9 oz | $2.40 |

Use the price graph you constructed to answer the following questions.

6. What is the price of 5 oz of Crunchy Crackers?

7. What is the price of 1 oz of Buzzy Tuna?

8. What is the price of 2 oz of Bessy's Pancake Mix?

9. What is the price of 14 oz of Pino's Imported Pasta?

10. What is the price of 15 oz of Lean Ground Beef?

## Writing

The information below is missing data that is needed to complete the problem. Tell what is missing. Make up data that could be used to complete and solve the problem.

11. The price of a box of biscuits is $0.89. On the box it says, "New larger size—15 ounces."

# Cheaper By the Pound

## Applying Skills

Find the price per pound to decide the better buy.

| Potatoes | |
|---|---|
| 2 lbs | $1.09 |
| 5 lbs | $2.69 |
| 10 lbs | $3.59 |
| 20 lbs | $6.29 |

**1.** What is the price per pound of each package of potatoes?

**2.** Which size package of potatoes is the best buy in terms of price per pound?

Calculate the price per pound of the items below.

| | Item | Price per Item | Weight in Pounds | Price per Pound |
|---|---|---|---|---|
| **3.** | Bike | $179.99 | 45 | |
| **4.** | Rollerblades | $135.99 | 11 | |
| **5.** | Basketball | $ 24.99 | 2 | |
| **6.** | 1996 complete set of baseball cards | $ 26.99 | 3.6 | |
| **7.** | Earrings | $ 16.00 | 0.25 | |
| **8.** | Watch | $ 34.95 | 0.25 | |
| **9.** | Pearl ring | $ 79.99 | 0.13 | |

**10.** For which of the items above would you pay the least per pound?

## Extending Concepts

**11.** Alejandro bought an 18-lb watermelon for $4.00. To the nearest cent, what is the price per pound?

**12.** A 5-lb bag of dog food sells for $3.85. Maurice's dog eats 2 bags of dog food every month. What is the monthly price per pound of the dog food?

## Making Connections

**13.** Select several magazines or newspapers. Find out how much a subscription costs to each of the magazines or newspapers. Compare the unit price to the newsstand price.

# It Really Adds Up

## Applying Skills

| Crunchy Popcorn | No-Ad Popcorn |
|-----------------|---------------|
| $0.45 per bag | $0.35 per bag |

Find the price of buying one bag of popcorn every day for a week.

**1.** Crunchy Popcorn

**2.** No-Ad Popcorn

Find the price of buying one bag of popcorn every day for a month (4.3 weeks).

**3.** Crunchy Popcorn

**4.** No-Ad Popcorn

Find the price of buying one bag of popcorn every day for a year.

**5.** Crunchy Popcorn

**6.** No-Ad Popcorn

**7.** How much would you save if you bought No-Ad Popcorn instead of Crunchy Popcorn for:

  **a.** 1 week

  **b.** 1 month (4.3 weeks)

  **c.** 1 year

**8.** If you bought a bag of No-Ad Popcorn every day instead of Crunchy Popcorn, how many days would it take to save $30? $75? Explain how you figured it out.

## Extending Concepts

**9.** At Jacy's Market, you can get 5 mangos for $1.95. At Nia's Market, you can get 3 for $1.29. Are the mangos cheaper at Jacy's or at Nia's?

**10.** You can get 3 cans of Mei Mei's Soup for $1.23 and 2 cans of Pei's Soup for $0.84. Which brand is the least per can?

**11.** Why would a store owner price an item at $9.99 for 5 instead of $2.00 each?

## Making Connections

**12.** Select two supermarket advertisements from a newspaper. Compare the prices of similar items. Which store seems to have the better buys? Give reasons for your answer.

# Dancing Ratios

## Applying Skills

Write each ratio as a fraction in lowest terms.

**1.** 6 to 8      **2.** 8:44      **3.** $\dfrac{60}{32}$

Write two equal ratios for each of the ratios below.

**4.** 5:30      **5.** 26:13      **6.** 12:36

**7.** Kirti developed a roll of 36 prints from the dance. Twenty-seven turned out well. What is the ratio of good prints to bad prints?

**8.** Arturo videotaped the dance for 1 hour and 40 minutes. He used a 3-hour videotape. Write the ratio of used tape to total tape.

## Extending Concepts

The data below show how some students spent their time from 4 P.M. to 5 P.M. yesterday. Decide if statements **9–12** are true or false.

**How Students Spent Their Time**

| | Number of Students |
|---|---|
| Homework | 𝍸𝍸 𝍸𝍸 |
| Sports practice | 𝍸𝍸 |
| Music practice | 𝍸𝍸 |
| Chores or job | 𝍸𝍸 l |
| Other | llll |

**9.** One out of every three students did homework.

**10.** One out of every five students did chores.

**11.** The ratio of students doing homework to students practicing music is 5 to 2.

**12.** The ratio of students doing chores to students practicing music or sports is 2 to 3.

## Making Connections

**13.** Sports statistics use ratios to describe a player's performance. Choose several players in a sport you enjoy. Research the players' statistics and write several ratios for each set of statistics. For example, baseball ratios might include hits to at bats or total bases to hits. Football ratios could include field goals made to field goals attempted.

Compare the ratios for players you have chosen. Do the ratios explain why one player is more valuable than another?

# Which Brand Has the Most Chocolate?

## Applying Skills

Write = or ≠ for each pair of ratios.

**1.** $\frac{3}{4}, \frac{9}{16}$

**2.** $\frac{4}{6}, \frac{6}{9}$

**3.** $\frac{8}{4}, \frac{10}{5}$

**4.** $\frac{20}{16}, \frac{15}{12}$

| Awesome Snack Mix | Crunchy Snack Mix |
|---|---|
| 8 oz chocolate chips | 4 oz chocolate chips |
| 6 oz peanuts | 2 oz peanuts |

**5.** What is the ratio of chocolate chips to peanuts in Awesome Snack Mix?

**6.** What is the ratio of chocolate chips to peanuts in Crunchy Snack Mix?

**7.** Are the ratios of chocolate chips to peanuts in Awesome Snack Mix and Crunchy Snack Mix the same or different?

**8.** Which contains more chocolate per ounce: Awesome Snack Mix or Crunchy Snack Mix? Note: The mixes contain only peanuts and chocolate chips.

Use cross products to compare ratios. Write = or ≠ for each blank.

**9.** $\frac{4}{6}$ ___ $\frac{5}{10}$

**10.** $\frac{2}{5}$ ___ $\frac{4}{106}$

**11.** $\frac{4}{8}$ ___ $\frac{4}{16}$

**12.** $\frac{2}{3}$ ___ $\frac{6}{12}$

## Extending Concepts

Use the given numbers to write equal ratios.

**13.** 3, 5, 9, 15

**14.** 1, 6, 6, 36

**15.** Find a ratio that is equal to $\frac{64}{72}$.

**16.** Find two odd numbers between 30 and 50 that have a ratio of 7 : 5.

## Making Connections

**17.** Use a cookbook or other reference book to find the number of calories in one medium-size pear, peach, apple, orange, plum, and nectarine. Compare the calories in the fruits by writing them as ratios.

**39**

# Halftime Refreshments

## Applying Skills

Four spoonfuls of lemonade mix make 2 cups of lemonade. Write a proportion to show how many spoonfuls of lemonade mix would be needed for each quantity of lemonade:

**1.** 22 cups    **2.** 46 cups    **3.** 68 cups

**Is each a proportion? Write *yes* or *no*.**

**4.** $\dfrac{48}{84} = \dfrac{4}{7}$

**5.** $\dfrac{15}{18} = \dfrac{20}{24}$

**6.** $\dfrac{5}{4} = \dfrac{24}{20}$

**7.** $\dfrac{9}{7} = \dfrac{27}{28}$

**Solve each proportion. Use cross products or equal ratios.**

**8.** $\dfrac{n}{6} = \dfrac{6}{9}$

**9.** $\dfrac{1}{3} = \dfrac{n}{18}$

**10.** $\dfrac{15}{3} = \dfrac{n}{8}$

**11.** $\dfrac{15}{n} = \dfrac{10}{16}$

## Extending Concepts

**12.** How many proportions can you make using only the numbers 1, 3, 4, 9, and 12?

**13.** Hot chocolate sold at a ratio of 3 to 1 compared to brownies at the football game. If 500 total items were sold, how many hot chocolates and how many brownies were sold?

## Making Connections

**14.** Hindu merchants used a method similar to proportion when pricing their products. A sample problem is: "If 12 palas of saffron is 18 niskas, what is the price of 36 palas?" Make a proportion for this problem. Use the information from the problem to write several other proportions.

# A Proportional Buffet

## Applying Skills

### Asian Pork Stir Fry

| | |
|---|---|
| 8 oz spinach linguine | 10 oz pork tenderloin, sliced |
| 3 oz soy sauce | 4 oz shiitake mushrooms, sliced |
| 2 tablespoons rice vinegar | 6 oz water |
| 1 tablespoon cornstarch | 1 large red pepper, sliced |
| 3 teaspoons sugar | 5 carrots, sliced |
| 1 tablespoon peanut oil | 2 green onions, sliced |
| 2 garlic cloves, thinly sliced | 7 broccoli florets |
| 1 tablespoon ginger root, minced | |

Makes 8 servings

Use proportions to increase the recipe to serve 20 people. How much of each ingredient will be needed?

1. spinach linguine
2. soy sauce
3. rice vinegar
4. cornstarch
5. sugar
6. peanut oil
7. garlic cloves
8. ginger root
9. pork tenderloin
10. mushrooms
11. water
12. red peppers
13. carrots
14. green onions
15. broccoli

## Extending Concepts

16. Taktuk is making fruit punch for the International Dinner. To make the punch he must mix 1 part concentrate to 4 parts water. He mixed 60 mL of concentrate and 240 mL of water. Did he use the correct proportion? Explain.

17. There are onions and green peppers in a bag. The ratio of onions to green peppers is 8 to 19. How many total vegetables are in the bag if there are 40 onions?

## Making Connections

18. Find the circumference of a basketball. Find out the sizes of at least three other game balls used in sports. Write and solve proportions to compare the circumferences of the balls.

# Team Spirit

## Applying Skills

The field hockey team's total expenses for last year were $10,000. Estimate how much was spent on each of the expenses listed below. Use benchmarks and mental math to make your estimates.

| | Item | Percent of Budget | Estimated Cost |
|---|---|---|---|
| **1.** | Uniforms | 22% | |
| **2.** | Transportation | 4% | |
| **3.** | Coach's Salary | 12% | |
| **4.** | Equipment | 49% | |
| **5.** | Officials' Fees | 6% | |
| **6.** | Trainer's Salary | 7% | |

Estimate each number in items **7–10.** Then use your calculator to see how close your estimate is.

**7.** 49% of 179

**8.** 24% of 319

**9.** 19% of 354

**10.** 34% of 175

**11.** Find 7% of $400.

7% means_____ for every_____

**12.** Find 12% of $300

12% means_____ for every_____

## Extending Concepts

**13.** To estimate 24% of 43, LeRon substituted numbers and found 25% of 44. His answer was 11. Using his calculator, he found that the exact answer is 10.32. LeRon concluded that substituting numbers causes you to overestimate. Do you agree? If not, give a counterexample.

**14.** Nirupa calls home from college at least once a week. A 30-minute phone call costs $10.00 on weekdays. Nirupa can save 20% if she calls on a weekend. How much money does she save on a 30-minute call made on Saturday?

## Making Connections

**15.** Look through newspapers and magazines to find articles involving percents. Design a collage with the articles. Write out percents from 1 through 100 and their equivalent fractional benchmarks.

# Playing Around

## Applying Skills

The circle graph below shows the budget for the middle school production of *Once Upon a Mattress*.

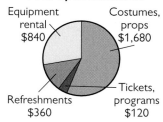

**Budget for**
**Once Upon a Mattress**

Equipment rental $840

Costumes, props $1,680

Refreshments $360

Tickets, programs $120

Use the circle graph to estimate what percent of the total cost was spent on each of the following:

**1.** costumes and props

**2.** tickets and programs

**3.** refreshments

**4.** equipment rental

Use your calculator to help you find the actual percent of the total cost that was spent on each of the following:

**5.** costumes and props

**6.** tickets and programs

**7.** refreshments

**8.** equipment rental

Use the following information to make a circle graph.

**9.** Ticket sales for *Once Upon a Mattress* totaled $560. Students collected the following amounts: Vanessa $168, Kimiko $140, Ying $112, Felicia $84, and Norma $56. Label the circle graph, using names and the percents collected. Give the graph a title.

## Extending Concepts

Step-in-Time shoe store took in the following amounts in January:

| | |
|---|---|
| Men's dress shoes | $750 |
| Women's dress shoes | $1,500 |
| Children's sneakers | $2,000 |
| Adult athletic shoes | $850 |

The circle graph below was made using the information above.

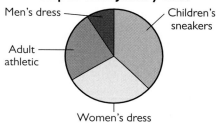

**Step-in-Time January Sales**

Men's dress

Children's sneakers

Adult athletic

Women's dress

**10.** Was the circle graph made correctly? Explain.

## Making Connections

**Percentage of the World's Population by Continent**

| | |
|---|---|
| Africa | 12% |
| Europe | 14% |
| North America | 8% |
| Asia | 60% |
| South America | 6% |

Source: *World Almanac 1996*

**11.** Use the handout Circle Graph to make a circle graph of the world's population.

# Sale Daze

## Applying Skills

Use a calculator to find the discount and sale price for items 1–4. Round to the nearest cent.

1. regular price: $78
   rate of discount: 25%

2. regular price: $29
   rate of discount: 20%

3. regular price: $45
   rate of discount: 15%

4. regular price: $120
   rate of discount: 37%

**Which shop has the better buy?**

| | Item | Super Sports | Sammy's Sport Shop |
|---|---|---|---|
| **5.** | Football | Regular price: $39.95 rate of discount: 10% | Regular price: $42.95 rate of discount: 15% |
| **6.** | Basketball | Regular price: $36.50 rate of discount: 20% | Regular price: $35 rate of discount: 15% |
| **7.** | Helmet | Regular price: $19.95 rate of discount: 20% | Regular price: $17.95 rate of discount: 15% |

8. Orit needed a helmet to skate on the half-pipe at Skateboard Plaza. She bought one for 60% off the regular price of $31.50. How much did she save? How much did she pay?

9. Salvador paid $27.50 for a catcher's mask that was on sale. The regular price was $36.90. What was the discount?

## Extending Concepts

10. Kai-Ju has saved $40 to buy a tennis racket that regularly sells for $59.99. She read an ad that announced a 25% discount on the racket. Has she saved enough money to buy it? If so, how much will she have left over? If not, how much more does she need?

11. Ryan went into a hardware store that had a 20%-off sale. His two purchases originally had prices of $38.75 and $7.90. How much did Ryan save because of the sale?

## Writing

Make up the missing data in items 12 and 13. Then write a word problem that can be solved using the data.

12. roller skates
    regular price: $89.99
    rate of discount:

13. tennis racket
    regular price: $45.89
    rate of discount:

# Percent Smorgasbord

## Applying Skills

For items **1–4**, how many items on the list can the shopper buy without overspending?

**1.** shopper has $140
discount: 12%

| | |
|---|---|
| video game set | $89.95 |
| video game cartridge | $29.50 |
| blow dryer | $27.50 |
| sweater | $34.00 |

**2.** shopper has $150
discount: 10%

| | |
|---|---|
| roller skates | $99.00 |
| compact disk | $12.99 |
| jacket | $75.00 |
| shirt | $18.00 |

**3.** shopper has $180
discount: 25%

| | |
|---|---|
| bicycle | $129.00 |
| bike helmet | $ 39.00 |
| tennis racket | $ 89.00 |
| ring | $ 58.00 |

**4.** shopper has $62
discount: 50%

| | |
|---|---|
| radio | $29.00 |
| jeans | $32.00 |
| earrings | $18.00 |
| shoes | $44.00 |

**5.** A box of Munchy Cereal contains 24 oz of cereal. It is on sale for 50% off the regular price of $4.80. Toasty Cereal, which contains 50% more cereal than Munchy Cereal, is $4.80 per box.

Which box has the lower price per ounce? To the nearest cent, how much less is the price per ounce for this box?

## Extending Concepts

Use your calculator to find the total for each bill. The tip is 15%.

**6.** **South of the Border**

| | |
|---|---|
| Beef tacos | $6.25 |
| Guacamole | $4.50 |
| Chicken tamale | $7.50 |

**7.** **Thai Cuisine**

| | |
|---|---|
| Chicken with ginger | $7.95 |
| Sweet and sour chicken | $8.90 |
| Shrimp and baby corn | $9.95 |

## Writing

**8.** Answer the letter to Dr. Math.

> Dear Dr. Math,
> Neely's Hot Dogs advertises that their hot dogs contain more protein than fat. Their hot dogs contain proteins, carbohydrates, and fat. Each hot dog contains 11 g of fat and 2 g of carbohydrates. This makes up 55% of the hot dog's content. Could the advertisement be true? How can I tell?
> Lois Kallory

**45**

# STUDENT GALLERY

Save with coupons

compare cost

Compare quantities

estimate
expenses

budget

The Seeing and Thinking Mathematically project is based at Education Development Center, Inc. (EDC), Newton, MA, and was supported, in part, by the National Science Foundation Grant No. 9054677. Opinions expressed are those of the authors and not necessarily those of the National Science Foundation.

CREDITS: Photography: Chris Conroy • Beverley Harper (cover) • Donald B. Johnson • © SuperStock: pp. 3TL, 3TM, 4, 14. Illustrations: Rob Blackard: pp. 6, 7, 10, 11, 30, 31.

© 1998 Creative Publications

Two Prudential Plaza, Suite 1175
Chicago, IL 60601

Printed in the United States of America.

0-7622-0217-3

4 5 6 7 8 9 10.02 01 00